Sam Leong

梁兆基

A Wok Through Time

Sam Leong 梁兆基

A Wok Through Time

Marshall Cavendish Cuisine

Chef: Sam Leong
Chef's Assistants: Chef Krisna B. and Chef Thomas Chai
Photographer: Joyce Choo

First published (cased with jacket) 2004
This limp edition 2009

Copyright © 2004 Marshall Cavendish International (Asia) Private Limited

Published by Marshall Cavendish Cuisine
An imprint of Marshall Cavendish International
1 New Industrial Road, Singapore 536196

Limits of Liability/Disclaimer of Warranty: The Author and Publisher of this book have used their best efforts in preparing
this book. The Publisher makes no representation or warranties with respect to the contents of this book and is not
responsible for the outcome of any recipe in this book. While the Publisher has reviewed each recipe carefully, the reader
may not always achieve the results desired due to variations in ingredients, cooking temperatures and individual cooking
abilities. The Publisher shall in no event be liable for any loss of profit or any other commercial damage,
including but not limited to special, incidental, consequential, or other damages.

Other Marshall Cavendish Offices:
Marshall Cavendish Ltd.5th Floor, 32–38 Saffron Hill, London EC1N 8FH · Marshall Cavendish Corporation.
99 White Plains Road, Tarrytown NY 10591-9001, USA · Marshall Cavendish International (Thailand) Co Ltd.
253 Asoke, 12th Flr, Sukhumvit 21 Road, Klongtoey Nua, Wattana, Bangkok 10110, Thailand
· Marshall Cavendish (Malaysia) Sdn Bhd, Times Subang, Lot 46, Subang Hi-Tech Industrial Park,
Batu Tiga, 40000 Shah Alam, Selangor Darul Ehsan, Malaysia

Marshall Cavendish is a trademark of Times Publishing Limited

National Library Board Singapore Cataloguing in Publication Data

Leong, Sam, 1966-
A wok through time / Sam Leong ; [chef's assistants, Krisna B. and Thomas Chai].
– Singapore : Marshall Cavendish Cuisine, 2009.
p. cm.
ISBN-13 : 978-981-261-671-5 (pbk.)
ISBN-10 : 981-261-671-3 (pbk.)

1. Cookery, Chinese. I. Krisna B. II. Chai, Thomas. III. Title.

TX724.5.C5
641.5951 -- dc22   OCN259866124

Printed in Singapore by Times Graphics Pte Ltd

Contents

MY DAD THE CHEF

Contents

COOKING FOR VIPs AND CELEBRITIES

Contents

Foreword

Singapore is a gourmet city. Tourists flock to our shores for spicy food, vegetables cooked Chinese style and seafood fresh from the oceans of our region. As for locals, they love food so much that dinner conversations often focus on the next meal.

Yet, excellent food is not possible without excellent chefs. In this regard, Sam Leong stands tall among the best. Locally, he is recognised as a key creator of New Asian Cuisine as well as a mentor and master to many young chefs. Internationally, he is recognised for his ability to blend the flavours of common and exotic ingredients to create sensational new tastes, showcase Chinese dishes in a way that rivals the elegance of fine French and Japanese cuisine, and create a table that is as magical as a spa experience. This is how I would describe Sam's talent; others may describe it differently, but I am sure all who know Sam will agree that a totally unique quality prevails in the way that he creates and presents traditional Chinese food.

Through the many recipes and beautiful photographs in this book, the genius of this master chef blossoms forth. This book required a lot of hard work to put together, including years of experimentation by Sam in the kitchen. Fortunately, our task as book and food lovers is simply to enjoy the flavours, the romance and the uniqueness of the culinary creations he has showcased here for us.

Mrs Pamelia Lee
International Tourism Consultant

Dedication

To my wife, Forest Leong, whose
love and encouragement has
enabled me to pursue my career
to the utmost.

To Andrew Tjioe,
the CEO of the Tung Lok
Group, who has given me
countless opportunities in the
advancement of my career.

Acknowledgement

I would like to thank all my **friends and guests** who have supported me through the years, helping me to win the Asian Ethnic Chef of the Year title at the World Gourmet Summit Awards of Excellence in 2001, 2002 and 2004.

MY DAD
THE CHEF

My grandfather left China and arrived in Malaysia during WWII because of poverty and a lack of job opportunities in the motherland. He believed that life in another country would be much better than staying put in China.

His hope to provide his large family with a more comfortable lifestyle, however, was met with great disappointment. Many immigrant workers who fled the motherland at that time had to endure harsh working environments, physical abuse from employers and long working hours with little to eat.

My dad, who was very young then, decided that the best thing to do was to work in a kitchen because food would be constantly available and he would not go hungry! His determination encouraged the rest of the family to join him and learn to become cooks. In time to come, his fierce determination also garnered him the reputation of being one of the best Chinese chefs in Kuala Lumpur in the 1960s.

FAREWELL PARTY TO
CHEF LEONG

My dad started working as a restaurant server when he was just 12 years old, but quickly became a chef because of his sheer determination to succeed. He worked with my uncle at the Tai Thong Restaurant in KL for a number of years before making a name for himself in KL's first hotel, the Merlin Hotel, in the 1960s before moving on to the Equatorial Hotel. Subsequently, he opened his own restaurant in KL and then Singapore. It was then that he decided to move his family to Singapore in 1980.

He spent a lot of time learning to create interesting dishes and improving on the existing ones. Whenever he had a day off from work, he would eat at other restaurants to try out their specialties so he could learn from them. He received much praise from veteran chefs as well as diners who patronised the establishments where he worked. Because of his charisma and determination to succeed, he also earned the nickname "Shark's Fin Soon" after his own name, Leong Mun Soon.

Although my dad loved to cook, he was not willing to do so at home. He left that task to my mum because he felt that domestic cooking was not challenging enough for him. As a result, my mum picked up many great cooking tips from my dad.

Gradually, I also began to take an interest in cooking especially since I did not excel academically. It was then that my father decided to train me as a cook, very much to my delight.

Through my dad's tough training and supervision, I managed to pick up the cooking regime quickly. As I was willing to put in a lot of time and effort in learning the basics, I was soon given the responsibility of running a small section of the kitchen brigade.

"From watching my father,
I learnt to be a responsible family man."

Braised
Shark's Fin <small>with</small>
Crab Meat <small>and</small> Crab Roe

Serves 1

Ingredients

Shark's fin (*jin san kuo*)	80 g (10–12.5 cm piece)
Cooking oil	1 Tbsp
Chicken consommé*	150 ml + extra for blanching crab roe
Salt	1/2 tsp
Ground white pepper	a dash
Chinese cooking wine (*hua tiao*)	1 Tbsp
Corn flour (cornstarch)	1 tsp, mixed with 2 tsp water
Fresh crab roe	10 g

Garnish

Chervil	5 g

Method

- Prepare shark's fin. Steam shark's fin for 4 hours then soak in cold water overnight. Leave shark's fin in soaking liquid and steam for 2 hours then drain. Set aside on a serving plate.
- Heat some oil in a wok, put in chicken consommé and season to taste with salt, pepper and Chinese cooking wine. Thicken with corn flour mixture and pour onto prepared shark's fin.
- Poach crab roe with extra chicken consommé, then drain and arrange on top of shark's fin. Garnish with chervil.

*Chicken Consommé

Ingredients

Water	4 litres
Chicken	1 kg
Lean pork	750 g
Chinese (Yunnan) ham	330 g

Method

- Bring water to the boil and add chicken, lean pork and ham. Simmer over low heat for 8 hours or until about 2 litres of stock is left in the pot. Strain stock and discard ingredients.

Double-boiled
Winter Melon Consommé
with Shark's Fin and Seafood

Serves 2

Ingredients

Shark's fin (*jin san kuo*)	20 g
Winter melon	1, about 400 g
Prawns (shrimp)	40 g, poached, shelled and diced
Fresh crab meat	40 g, poached
Scallops	40 g, diced
Dried scallops	20 g, steamed (see Chef's Note) and shredded
Cooking oil	1 Tbsp
Chicken consommé	250 ml (page 24)
Salt	$1/_2$ tsp
Ground white pepper	a dash
Chinese cooking wine (*hua tiao*)	1 tsp

Garnish

Chinese wolfberries (*gou qi zi*)	6
Chinese (Yunnan) ham	5 g, finely minced

Method

- Prepare shark's fin (page 24).
- Slice cap off winter melon. Remove and discard seeds. Fill with cold water and stand in a heatproof bowl large enough to hold the melon. Steam for 15 minutes until melon is soft. Drain water.
- Place prawns, crab meat, fresh and dried scallops and shark's fin in melon. Set aside.
- Heat oil in a wok. Add chicken consommé and season to taste with salt, pepper and Chinese cooking wine. Pour into melon and steam for 10 minutes. Garnish with Chinese wolfberries and minced ham.

Chef's Note:

- To prepare dried scallops, soak them in cold water overnight. Drain and add enough chicken consommé to cover scallops, 2 slices ginger, 1 chopped spring onion and 1 tsp cooking oil. Steam for 45 minutes. Use scallops together with the liquid it was steamed in. This liquid is known as scallop jus.
- Chinese wolfberries are good for the liver, lung and kidney channels. It enriches yin, brightens the eyes and moistens the lungs. It is commonly used to treat anaemia, lower back aches, vision problems and long term coughs.

Steamed
Shark's Fin with
Yunnan Ham and Chinese Herbs
Wrapped in Fragrant Lotus Leaf

Serves 2

Ingredients

Shank's fin (*jin san kuo*)	80 g (10–12.5 cm piece)
Chinese (Yunnan) ham	10 g, julienned
Chinese wolfberries (*gou qi zi*)	6
Fragrant Solomonseal rhizome (*yu zhu*)	5 g
Cooking oil	1 Tbsp
Chicken consommé	150 ml (page 24)
Salt	$1/2$ tsp
Chinese cooking wine (*hua tiao*)	1 Tbsp
Corn flour (cornstarch)	1 tsp, mixed with 2 tsp water
Lotus leaf	1

Method

- Prepare lotus leaf 1–2 weeks in advance. Poach in hot water then dry completely. Place between 2 sheets of paper large enough to cover leaf then flatten with weights such as books. Leave for 1–2 weeks to achieve a lovely brown coloured leaf.
- Prepare shark's fin (page 24).
- In a heatproof dish, place prepared shark's fin topped with ham, wolfberries and Solomonseal. Steam for 10 minutes.
- Meanwhile, heat some oil in a wok, add chicken consommé and season to taste with salt and Chinese cooking wine. Thicken with corn flour mixture.
- Carefully transfer shark's fin onto lotus leaf and pour sauce over ingredients to serve.

Chef's Note:

- Fragrant Solomonseal rhizome (*yu zhu*) is good for the lungs and stomach channels. It nourishes yin, prevents internal dryness, extinguishes wind and softens the sinews. It is commonly used to treat irritability, thirst, sensation of heat in the bones and cramped and hard muscles.

Stewed
Dong Po
Pork Belly

Serves 1

Ingredients

Pork belly	100 g
Ginger	1 slice
Nutmeg	1
Star anise	$^{1}/_{2}$
Lotus seeds	5 g, soaked overnight
Onion	10 g, peeled and sliced
Rock sugar	10 g
Dark mushroom soy sauce	2 tsp
Chinese cooking wine (*hua tiao*)	40 ml
Chicken consommé	70 ml (page 24)
Corn flour (cornstarch)	1 tsp, mixed with 2 tsp water

Method

- Cut pork belly into cubes and use the broad side of a knife to pat and smoothen skin. Scald pork belly with boiling water.
- Put all ingredients except corn flour into a clay pot and fill with enough water to cover pork belly.
- Bring to the boil over high heat then reduce heat and simmer for 3 hours until ingredients are soft and fragrant. Thicken sauce with corn flour mixture.

Steamed Rice with
Diced Chicken in
Fermented Black Bean Sauce *Serves 1*

Ingredients

Freshly steamed rice	100 g
Boneless chicken drumstick	50 g, diced
Salt	to taste
Sugar	$1/2$ tsp
Egg white	$1/2$
Corn flour (cornstarch)	$1/4$ tsp + 1 tsp, mixed with 2 tsp water
Sesame oil	$1/4$ tsp
Cooking oil	1 Tbsp
Spring onion (scallion)	5 g, chopped
Ginger	5 g, peeled and sliced
Fresh button mushroom	5 g, sliced
Red chillies	5 g, diced
Chicken consommé	40 ml (page 24)
Fermented black bean sauce	1 tsp
Oyster sauce	2 tsp
Sugar	1 tsp
Chinese cooking wine (*hua tiao*)	5 tsp

Garnish
Roasted white sesame seeds

Method
- Press hot steamed rice into a ring cutter to form a rice patty. Set aside on a serving plate.
- Marinate diced chicken with salt, sugar, egg white, $1/4$ tsp corn flour and sesame oil. Heat cooking oil in a wok and sear chicken lightly.
- Add remaining ingredients except corn flour mixture and sesame seeds to wok. Sauté for a few minutes until chicken is cooked. Thicken with corn flour mixture and pour over rice patty. Garnish with sesame seeds.

Chef's Note:
- Use freshly steamed hot rice so that the rice patty will continue to hold its shape even after the sauce is poured over it.

Roasted
Pork Shank with
Chinese Herbs *Serves 2*

Ingredients

Pork shank	600 g
Potato flour	40 g
Cooking oil for deep-frying	
Carrots	100 g, sliced
Daikon (Japanese radish)	100 g, sliced
Onions	100 g, peeled and sliced
Cabbage	100 g, chopped
Chinese celery	10 g, chopped
Salted fish	10 g, diced
Chicken consommé	200 ml (page 24)
Cooking oil	1 Tbsp
Yellow bean sauce	3 Tbsp
Red chillies	2, finely diced
Sugar	3 tsp
Chinese cooking wine (*hua tiao*)	5 tsp

Method

- Preheat oven to 65°C.
- Dust pork shank with potato flour. Heat oil for deep-frying and deep-fry pork shanks until golden brown. Drain well.
- Combine pork shank and all other ingredients in a pot and simmer over very low heat for 4 hours. Transfer shanks onto a baking tray and bake for 25 minutes. Serve.

Julienned
Chicken with Yunnan Ham
in Chicken Consommé

Serves 1

Ingredients

Chinese (Yunnan) ham	40 g, julienned
Chicken breast	120 g, cooked and finely shredded
Cooking oil	1 Tbsp
Chicken consommé	120 ml (page 24)
Spinach	a few leaves
Salt	$1/4$ tsp
Sugar	$1/4$ tsp
Chinese cooking wine (*hua tiao*)	$1/4$ tsp
Ground white pepper	a dash

Method

- Place ham on chicken shreds and steam for 2 minutes. Arrange in the centre of a serving plate.
- Heat oil in a wok and add chicken consommé and spinach leaves. Bring to the boil and season with salt, sugar, Chinese cooking wine and pepper. Spoon over ham and chicken to serve.

Warm
Glutinous Rice with
Sautéed Minced Beef

Serves 1

Ingredients

Glutinous rice	100 g
Cooking oil	1 Tbsp
Minced beef	30 g
Red chillies	2, minced

Seasoning

Salt	¹/₄ tsp
Sugar	¹/₄ tsp
Oyster sauce	1 tsp
Dark soy sauce	¹/₄ tsp
Sesame oil	¹/₄ tsp
Ground white pepper	a dash

Garnish
Chives

Method

- Soak glutinous rice in cold water overnight. Drain and steam for 20 minutes.
- Heat oil in a wok and sauté minced beef. Add chillies, glutinous rice and seasoning.
- Spoon glutinous rice into a bowl and steam for 10 minutes. Serve garnished with chives.

Wok-fried **Radish Cakes** with **Yellow Chives** and **Bean Sprouts** in Homemade **Dry XO Sauce**

Serves 1

Ingredients

Cooking oil	1 Tbsp
Yellow chives	5 g
Bean sprouts	5 g
Oyster sauce	$^1/_2$ tsp
Sugar	$^1/_4$ tsp
Dry XO sauce	$^1/_2$ tsp (page 148)
Chinese cooking wine (*hua tiao*)	$^1/_4$ tsp
Ground white pepper	a dash
Egg	1, beaten

Radish Cake

Water	500 ml
Glutinous rice flour	75 g
Potato flour	20 g
Corn flour (cornstarch)	20 g
Daikon (Japanese radish)	100 g, julienned and wok-fried
Dried prawns (shrimps)	20 g, minced and wok-fried
Fresh shiitake mushrooms	20 g, wok-fried
Chinese sausages	20 g, minced and wok-fried
Sugar	5 g
Salt	5 g

Method

- Prepare radish cake. Mix 250 ml water with glutinous rice flour, potato flour and corn flour.
- Mix remaining water with daikon, dried prawns, mushrooms, Chinese sausages, sugar and salt.
- Combine both mixtures and pour into a square baking tray. Steam for 35 minutes. Leave to cool before cutting into 3 x 3-cm pieces.
- Pan sear radish cake with a bit of oil. Add yellow chives and bean sprouts and sauté.
- Add oyster sauce, sugar, dry XO sauce, Chinese cooking wine and pepper and sauté. Pour in egg and sauté briskly. Serve.

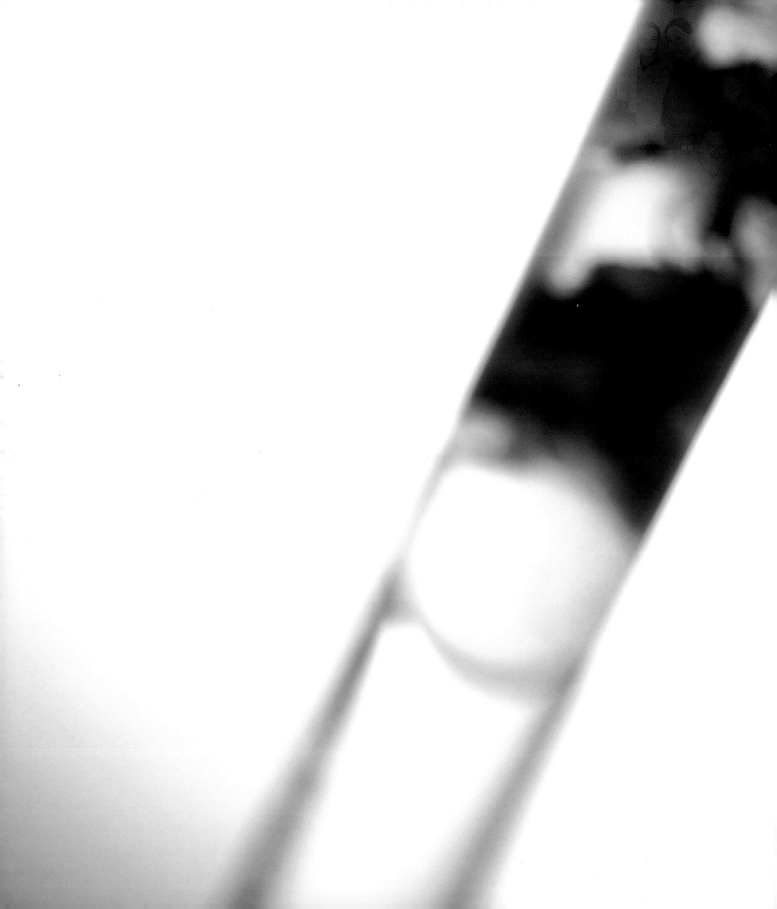

COOKING FOR
VIPs AND CELEBRITIES

It has been my great honour and privilege to be able to cook for many important people including Singapore's Minister Mentor Lee Kuan Yew, Singapore's Senior Minister Goh Chok Tong and former president of the USA, Bill Clinton.

I have also met with many famous international chefs like Wolfgang Puck, Charlie Trotter, Jean Georges Vongerichten and Nobu in the course of my work. I make an effort to meet up with them whenever I have the opportunity to travel to Europe or the USA, and I am glad that we have become good friends.

Crispy
Lobster Tempura
in Tom Yam Jus

Serves 1

Ingredients

Nori (dried seaweed)	1 sheet, sliced into 3 strips
Lobster meat	80 g, steamed
Asparagus	10 g, cut into 4-cm lengths
Avocado	10 g, sliced, pitted and julienned
Carrot	10 g, julienned
Corn flour (cornstarch)	
Cooking oil for deep-frying	

Tom Yam Jus

Chicken consommé	350 ml (page 24)
Sugar	2 Tbsp
Thai fish sauce	2 Tbsp
Tom yam paste	2 Tbsp
Chilli oil	$^1/_2$ Tbsp
Lemon grass	1 stalk
Kaffir lime leaf	1
Galangal	1 slice
Bird's eye chilli	1
Whipping cream	2 Tbsp
Lemon juice	2 Tbsp

Method

- Combine all tom yam jus ingredients except for lemon juice and bring to the boil for 20 minutes until fragrant and thick. Stir in lemon juice.
- Lay a strip of nori flat on a work surface and top with lobster meat, asparagus, avocado and carrot. Roll up tightly then continue to make another 2 rolls.
- Heat oil in a wok. Sprinkle nori rolls with corn flour and deep-fry until crisp and golden brown. Drain well.
- Arrange on a serving plate. Drizzle with tom yam jus and serve.

Seared
King Scallops ^{with}
Asparagus Cream

Serves 1

Ingredients

Cooking oil	1 Tbsp
King scallops	3
Tomato	1, skinned, seeded and finely diced

Asparagus Cream Sauce

Asparagus	50 g, chopped and poached
Whipping cream	20 g
Water	200 ml
White wine	50 ml
Salt	$1/2$ tsp
Ground white pepper	a dash

Ground Nori

Nori (dried seaweed)	1 sheet, toasted and ground

Method

- Combine asparagus cream sauce ingredients and bring to the boil for 1 hour until sauce is reduced. Process in a blender and strain.
- Heat oil and sear scallops on both sides until golden brown.
- Pour some asparagus cream sauce on a serving plate. Arrange scallops on top and sprinkle diced tomato over. Garnish with ground nori.

Chef's Note:

- Store excess ground nori in a clean airtight container for future use.

Warm Poached
Marinated **Prawns**
with **Spicy Lime** Vinaigrette

Ingredients

King prawns (shrimps)	50 g, deveined and shelled with tails intact
Cherry tomatoes	2, diced

Seasoning

Freshly squeezed lemon juice	3 tsp
Honey	2 tsp
Sake	1 tsp
Miri	$^1/_2$ tsp
White vinegar	$^1/_2$ tsp
Yellow miso paste	$^1/_4$ tsp
Olive oil	$^1/_4$ tsp

Garnish

Nori (dried seaweed) strips
Daikon sprouts

Method

- Mix seasoning in a blender.
- Marinate prawns in seasoning together with diced tomatoes. Arrange on a plate and garnish with nori strips and daikon sprouts.

Braised
Spiny Lobster with
Saffron Consommé and
Steamed Glutinous Rice

Ingredients

Serves 2

Lobster

Spiny lobster	1, about 500 g
Cooking oil for deep-frying	
Saffron chicken consommé*	120 ml
Salt	1/4 tsp
Sugar	1/4 tsp
Chinese cooking wine (*hua tiao*)	1/2 tsp

Glutinous Rice

Cooking oil	1/2 tsp
Chinese sausage	10 g
Dried Chinese mushroom	5 g, soaked to soften
Coriander (cilantro) stems	5 g
Glutinous rice	30 g, soaked overnight and drained

Seasoning

Oyster sauce	1/2 tsp
Light soy sauce	1/2 tsp
Sugar	1/4 tsp
Sesame oil	1/4 tsp
Ground white pepper	a dash

Garnish

Chopped red chillies
Daikon sprouts

Method

- Cut lobster lengthwise in half, then separate head and body. Clean head and steam for 2 minutes until red and cooked. Dry and set aside.
- Prepare glutinous rice. Heat oil in a wok and sauté Chinese sausage, mushroom and coriander until fragrant. Add glutinous rice and sauté. Add seasoning and mix well.
- Spoon glutinous rice into lobster head halves and steam for 4 minutes.
- Heat oil for deep-frying and deep-fry lobster body until browned. This will take about 30 seconds.
- Drain all but 1/2 tsp oil and add saffron chicken consommé and lobster body. Season with salt, sugar and Chinese cooking wine. Simmer until sauce is reduced and thick.
- Garnish with red chilli and daikon sprouts.

*Saffron Chicken Consommé

Ingredients

Water	4 litres
Chicken	1 kg
Lean pork	750 g
Chinese (Yunnan) ham	330 g
Saffron strands	1/4 tsp

Method

- Bring water to the boil water and add chicken, lean pork and ham. Simmer over low heat for 8 hours or until only about 2 litres of stock is left in the pot.
- Stir in saffron strands until consommé changes to a yellow colour. Strain stock and discard ingredients.

Pig's Trotters Jello with
Edamame Beans and
Lotus Seeds

Serves 1

Ingredients

Pig's trotters	120 g
Ginger	1 slice
Nutmeg	1
Star anise	4 segments
Lotus seeds	5 g, soaked overnight
Onion	10 g, peeled and sliced
Rock sugar	10 g
Dark mushroom soy sauce	2 tsp
Chinese cooking wine (*hua tiao*)	40 ml
Chicken consommé	70 ml (page 24)

Seasoning

White vinegar	$\frac{1}{2}$ tsp
Tomato sauce	$\frac{1}{2}$ tsp
Rock sugar	3 g

Garnish

Edamame beans	10 g, blanched

Method

- Using a flame, lightly torch pig's trotters to remove any hair on skin.
- Fill a pot with water and bring to the boil with ginger. Carefully place trotters in to cook for 30 minutes. Remove trotters and discard water.
- Put all ingredients except chicken consommé and seasoning into a clay pot and fill with enough water to cover trotters. Bring to the boil over high heat then reduce heat and simmer for 2 hours until ingredients are soft and fragrant, and sauce is reduced and thickened.
- Serve with edamame beans.

Salmon,
Avocado, Mango
Spring Roll ⁱⁿ

Passion Fruit Vinaigrette

Serves 1

Ingredients

Vietnamese rice paper	1 sheet
Salmon fillet	40 g, julienned
Avocado	20 g
Mango	20 g

Seasoning

Passion fruit	2, sliced in half and flesh scooped out
Mango	$1/2$, peeled and blended into a puree
Lemon juice	$1/2$ tsp
Honey	1 tsp

Method

- Soak Vietnamese paper in cold water for 5 minutes. Drain and place on a flat work surface.
- Place salmon, avocado and mango on rice paper and wrap neatly. Slice in half and place on a serving plate.
- Combine seasoning ingredients and mix well. Drizzle over spring roll.

Pan-seared
Duck Breast Roll
Stuffed with Asparagus
in Light Soy Vinaigrette

Serves 1

Ingredients

Skinless duck breast	80 g, diced
Five-spice powder	1/4 tsp
Chinese cooking wine	
(*hua tiao*)	1/2 tsp
Oyster sauce	1 tsp
Ginger powder	1/4 tsp
Sugar	1/4 tsp
Corn flour (cornstarch)	1/4 tsp
Egg white	1/2
Asparagus	10 g, blanched
Cooking oil	1/2 tsp

Light Soy Vinaigrette

Black vinegar	200 ml
Ginger	3 slices
Brown sugar	40 g

Method

- Combine light soy vinaigrette ingredients and leave to simmer until reduced and thick.
- Using a blender, process duck breast with five-spice powder, Chinese cooking wine, oyster sauce, ginger powder, sugar, corn flour and egg white into a paste. Leave in the refrigerator to chill for 1 hour.
- Spread paste onto a clean plastic sheet and place asparagus in the centre. Roll up tightly and steam for 12 minutes.
- Remove plastic sheet and cut duck roll into 4-cm pieces. Heat oil in a pan and sear until lightly browned.
- Combine and heat ingredients for light soy vinaigrette until sugar is dissolved. Serve on the side with duck roll.

Baked
Fillet Cod Marinated with
Miso-Honey Accompanied with
Wasabi-pickled Cucumber

Serves 1

Ingredients
Cod fillet   100 g

Marinade
Red miso paste   60 g
Sugar   50 g
Sake   50 ml
Water   15 ml
Egg yolk   ¹/₂

Wasabi-pickled Cucumber
Cucumbers   50 g, thinly sliced
Sugar   200 g
Freshly grated wasabi   5 g, diluted with 1 Tbsp white vinegar
Water   160 ml
White vinegar   160 ml

Method
- Prepare pickled cucumber. Marinate cucumbers with sugar, wasabi, water and vinegar. Cover and refrigerate for 3 days.
- Marinate cod with combined marinade ingredients and leave overnight.
- Preheat oven to 180°C and bake cod for 15 minutes until crisp and golden brown. Arrange pickled cucumbers on a serving plate and place cod on top to serve.

New Style
Sashimi

Serves 1

Ingredients
Yellow tail fillet   100 g, thinly sliced

Sauce
Warm cooking oil   1 tsp
Light soy sauce   1 tsp
Black vinegar $^1/_2$ tsp
Brown sugar $^1/_2$ tsp, dissolved in 2 tsp water
Sesame oil $^1/_2$ tsp
Mirin $^1/_2$ tsp
Sake $^1/_2$ tsp
Red miso paste $^1/_4$ tsp
Garlic   5 g, peeled, roasted and minced

Method
- Combine sauce ingredients and mix well. Gently heat to warm it.
- Arrange yellow tail on a plate. Drizzle warmed sauce over fish. Garnish and serve.

Shanghainese
La Mian with
Sautéed Minced Pork

Serves 1

Ingredients

Shanghainese *la mian*	120 g

Sautéed Minced Pork

Cooking oil	1 Tbsp
Minced lean pork	50 g
Fresh shiitake mushroom	3 g
Shallot	3 g, peeled and minced
Garlic	3 g, peeled and minced
Ginger	3 g, peeled and minced
Spring onion (scallion)	3 g, minced
Red chillies	3 g, minced
Chicken consommé	30 ml (page 24)
Hot bean paste	1 tsp
Oyster sauce	1/2 tsp
Sugar	1/2 tsp
Ground white pepper	a dash
Corn flour (cornstarch)	1 tsp, mixed with 2 tsp water

Garnish
Coriander (cilantro)

Method

- Heat oil in a wok and sauté minced pork until fragrant. Add mushroom, shallot, garlic, ginger, spring onion and red chillies and sauté. Add chicken consommé, hot bean paste, oyster sauce, sugar and pepper. Thicken with corn flour. Set aside.
- Soak *la mian* in cold water for 10 minutes. Julienne and poach in hot water. Drain and arrange on a serving plate.
- Top *la mian* with minced pork and mushroom mixture. Garnish with coriander.

Chilled Black and White Sesame Mousse

Serves 1

Ingredients

Black sesame seeds	50 g
White sesame seeds	50 g
Whipping cream	200 ml
Fresh milk	300 ml
Sugar	300 g
Water	50 ml
Gelatine sheets	4, soaked in iced water to soften

Method

- Soak black and white sesame seeds separately overnight. Drain then process separately in a blender into smooth pastes.
- Combine whipping cream, milk, sugar and water and simmer.
- Strain softened gelatine sheets and stir into simmering milk mixture until melted.
- Divide milk mixture equally into 2 separate saucepans. Stir black sesame paste into one and white sesame paste into the other.
- Spoon alternate layers of black and white sesame paste into a martini glass, waiting for each layer to set before adding the next. You can also use shot glasses for smaller helpings.

Chef's Note:

- To prevent the gelatine-sesame paste from setting in the saucepan, warm it every once in a while.

"Compared to my father's generation, cooks are now expected to learn more. Then, the wok chef never left the wok and the chopper only chopped. Now, chefs must master the art of food presentation as well."

Lemon Grass Jello
with Mixed Assorted Fruits
and Lime Sorbet

Serves 1

Ingredients

Kiwi fruit	5 g, peeled and diced
Strawberry	5 g, stemmed and diced
Mint leaves	5 g
Barley	5 g
Dried sea olive jelly	5 g
Black grass jelly	5 g
Lime sorbet	1 scoop

Lemon Grass Jello

Water	1 litre
Sugar	180 g
Screwpine (*pandan*) leaves	40 g
Lemon grass	50 g
Pomelo leaves	3
Gelatine powder	7 g, mixed with 25 g sugar

Garnish

Black sesame seeds	
Peanuts	5 g, crushed
Mint leaves	

Method

- Prepare lemon grass jello. Combine water, sugar, screwpine leaves, lemon grass and pomelo leaves and bring to the boil for 30 minutes. Strain and mix in gelatine powder. Leave at room temperature to set then chill in the refrigerator.
- Combine lemon grass jello with kiwi fruit, strawberry, mint leaves, barley, dried sea olive jelly and black grass jelly.
- Spoon into a tall glass and top with a scoop of lime sorbet. Garnish with black sesame seeds, crushed peanuts and mint leaves.

Cream of Pumpkin, Coconut Ice Cream, Black Glutinous Rice and Mango

Serves 1

Ingredients

Yellow pumpkin	1, small
Sugar syrup*	2 tsp
Whipping cream	10 ml
Black glutinous rice	10 g, soaked in cold water overnight
Sugar	20 g
Water	300 ml
Mango	30 g, peeled and diced
Coconut ice cream	1 scoop

Method

- Steam whole pumpkin for about 15 minutes until soft. Cut in half then scrape out and discard seeds.
- Scrape out flesh and puree in a blender with sugar syrup and whipping cream. Chill in the refrigerator.
- Drain black glutinous rice and simmer with sugar and water until rice is soft and water is reduced.
- Place diced mango on a plate and drizzle with chilled pumpkin puree. Top with a scoop of coconut ice cream and black glutinous rice.

*Sugar Syrup

Ingredients

Water	75 ml
Sugar	150 g

Method

- Bring water and sugar to the boil, stirring until sugar dissolves. Leave to cool before using.

Strawberry
Chocolate
Fondue

Serves 1

Ingredients

Milk chocolate	200 g
Whipping cream	50 ml
Milk	50 ml
Butter	20 g
Strawberries	5, each sliced in half

Method

- Combine chocolate, whipping cream, milk and butter in a microwave-safe container and heat in a microwave oven on HIGH for 20 seconds. Stir and mix well. Return to the microwave oven and heat on HIGH for another 20 seconds.
- Serve melted chocolate with strawberries in separate containers. Dip strawberries into melted chocolate before eating.

BRINGING
MODERN
CHINESE CUISINE
TO THE WORLD

In traditional Chinese cooking, each dish is meticulously prepared in advance and then presented dramatically for the delight of diners. Unfortunately, the dish would then be taken away to be divided and served on individual plates, 'destroying' the presentation and losing the originality of the dish.

I wanted to change this although I knew there would be many obstacles. I began to introduce the concept of preparing and serving individually portioned dishes. It was very time consuming for the kitchen brigade to prepare each dish individually and be consistent with the presentation. There was also the difficulty of pricing the dishes and ultimately, convincing guests to accept the new concept. But I never gave up.

In 1996, I was given the opportunity to participate in a charitable event in Los Angeles, USA, organised by Wolfgang Puck, one of America's most influential chefs. The Singapore news media was immediately attracted to my representation for Singapore and upon my return, the new concept began to take flight.

Many invitations to take part in international food events started to flood in, giving me the opportunity to showcase my creations and leading me to achieve my utmost. The Singapore news media then began to recognise my contribution to the food and beverage industry. Regular guests at the restaurant where I worked as well as new guests also began to support me in my ventures.

I am happy that my determination and the sacrifices I have made to create awareness of modern Chinese cuisine have been fruitful. I hope to continue to expose modern Chinese cuisine creations internationally, without losing the cuisine's Asian heritage.

Tuna Tartar and Mango Salsa in Black Pepper-crusted Popiah Cones

Serves 1

Ingredients

Popiah Cones

Spring roll wrappers (*popiah* skin)	4 sheets
Corn flour (cornstarch)	1 Tbsp, mixed with 2 Tbsp water
Freshly ground black pepper	
Cooking oil for deep-frying	

Tuna Tartar and Mango Salsa

Mango	30 g, peeled and diced
Tomato	30 g, diced
Onion	20 g, peeled and diced
Cucumber	30 g, peeled and diced
Tuna	100 g, cut into cubes
Truffle oil	1 tsp
Salt	a dash
Freshly ground black pepper	a dash

Garnish

Black sesame seeds

Method

- Prepare *popiah* cones. Cut spring roll wrappers into 8 x 8-cm squares. Wrap each square around a cone-shaped steel mould and seal edges with corn flour mixture.
- Sprinkle black pepper along sealed edge of cones. The moisture from the corn flour mixture will help the black pepper adhere to the cone.
- Deep-fry cones until crisp and golden brown. Leave to drain.
- Prepare tuna tartar and mango salsa. Mix mango, tomato, onion and cucumber with tuna cubes. Toss with truffle oil and season with salt and black pepper.
- Fill *popiah* cones with tuna tartar and mango salsa. Sprinkle with black sesame seeds and serve.

Foie Gras Broth
with Crab Roe

Ingredientss

Foie gras paste	80 g
Chicken consommé	150 ml, chilled (page 24)
Cooking oil	1 Tbsp
Salt	1/2 tsp
Chinese cooking wine	
(*hua tiao*)	1 Tbsp
Whipping cream	100 ml
Corn flour (cornstarch)	1 tsp, mixed with 2 tsp water

Garnish
Crab roe
Crisp bread slices (see Chef's Note)

Method

- Combine foie gras paste with chilled chicken consommé in a blender and process until smooth.
- Heat oil in a wok and pour in foie gras broth. Bring to the boil and season with salt and Chinese cooking wine.
- Stir in whipping cream and thicken with corn flour mixture. Garnish with crab roe and serve with crisp bread slices.

Chef's Note:

- To make crisp bread slices, slice a crusty white loaf into thin slices. Brush with egg white and sprinkle with chopped coriander and salt. Bake at 40°C for about 15 minutes until golden brown and crisp.

Crispy
Chrysanthemum-shaped
Fish with Mango and
Sweet Chilli Sauce

Serves 1

Ingredients
Cod fillet	100 g
Tapioca flour	
Cooking oil for deep-frying	

Sweet Chilli Sauce
Red chillies	25 g, each sliced in half lengthwise
Garlic	25 g, peeled and minced
Coriander (cilantro) leaves	15 g, chopped
Water	50 ml
Honey	50 ml
Thai fish sauce	50 ml
Lemon juice	100 ml

Garnish
Daikon sprouts	
Young green mango	10 g, peeled and julienned
Carrot	5 g, julienned

Method
- Score fish fillet diagonally and repeat in the opposite direction, leaving skin to hold resulting cubes together. Dust fillet with tapioca flour.
- Heat oil for deep-frying and deep-fry fish until skin turns crisp and golden brown. Drain and set aside.
- Prepare sweet chilli sauce. Combine all sauce ingredients in pan and simmer until chillies and garlic are soft, stirring occasionally.
- Spoon some sweet chilli sauce over deep-fried fish. Garnish with daikon sprouts, mango and carrot to serve.

Deep-fried
Flaky Taro and
Scallop Rings in
Salted Egg Puree

Serves 1

Ingredients

Taro Paste

Boiling water	5 tsp
Wheat starch flour	2 Tbsp
Taro	150 g, peeled and cut into thick slices
Vegetable shortening	40 g
Salt	$1/4$ tsp
Sugar	$1/4$ tsp
Five-spice powder	$1/4$ tsp
Scallops	2, boiled
Cooking oil	200 ml

Sauce

Salted egg yolks	2, steamed and chopped
Chicken consommé	40 ml (page 24)
Salt	$1/4$ tsp
Sugar	$1/4$ tsp
Chinese cooking wine (*hua tiao*)	1 Tbsp
Corn flour (cornstarch)	1 tsp, mixed with 2 tsp water

Topping

Tomato	1, skinned, seeded and finely diced
Caviar	$1/2$ tsp

Garnish

Alfalfa sprouts

Method

- Prepare taro paste. Pour boiling water into flour and mix well into a paste. Steam taro for about 30 minutes until cooked. Use a fork to mash up the taro then add flour paste, vegetable shortening, salt, sugar and five-spice powder. Mix into a smooth paste.
- Divide taro paste into 2 portions and shape into balls. Press a scallop into the centre of each taro ball and mould round. Heat oil and deep-fry until taro rings are crisp and golden brown. Drain well.
- Place salted egg yolks with chicken consommé, salt, sugar and Chinese cooking wine in a pot. Bring to the boil and thicken with corn flour.
- Top taro rings with diced tomato and caviar. Drizzle sauce on the side of taro rings and serve garnished with alfalfa sprouts.

Seared
Spinach Scallops
with Wasabi Sauce

Serves 1

Ingredients

Spinach leaves	50 g, minced
Egg white	$^1/_2$
Corn flour (cornstarch)	1 tsp
Salt	$^1/_2$ tsp
Scallops	2

Wasabi Sauce

Green seaweed powder	1 tsp
Purple seaweed powder	1 tsp
White seaweed powder	1 tsp
Grated fresh wasabi	5 g
Daikon (Japanese radish)	50 g, peeled and pureed
Water	70 ml
Light soy sauce	2 tsp
Japanese rice vinegar	2 tsp
Sugar	2 tsp
Olive oil	3 Tbsp

Method

- Combine minced spinach leaves with egg white, corn flour and salt to form a pasty mixture. Press mixture onto the top of each scallop and sear on low heat until golden brown at the edges. Flip scallops over and sear other side until golden brown at the edges. Remove and drain well.
- Prepare wasabi sauce. Combine sauce ingredients in a pot and bring to the boil. Lower heat to a simmer and allow liquid to reduce until it reaches a syrup-like consistency. Drizzle over scallops to serve.

Half-poached
Salmon with Homemade
Pickled Red Chilli in
Superior Chicken Consommé

Serves 1

Ingredients

Salmon fillet   120 g, sliced and poached

Pickled Red Chilli
Red chillies   40 g, minced
White vinegar   20 ml
Salt   1^1/$_2$ Tbsp
Water   40 ml
Saffron chicken consommé*   80 ml (page 54)
Chinese cooking wine
  (*hua tiao*)   1 Tbsp
Ground white pepper   a dash

Garnish
Fried minced garlic

Method

- Seal minced red chillies, vinegar, 1 Tbsp salt and water in a plastic container and leave at room temperature for 1 week. This will remove the spiciness of the chillies.
- Heat pickled red chilli mixture in a wok together with chicken consommé and Chinese cooking wine. Season with pepper.
- Arrange salmon on a serving plate and pour pickled red chilli mixture over. Garnish with fried minced garlic.

Chilled
Tomato Soup
Sorbet

Serves 1

Ingredients

Tomatoes	120 g
Chicken consommé	100 ml, chilled (page 24)
Honey	20 ml
Lemon juice	10 ml
Mirin	30 ml
Sake	30 ml
Salt	$^1/_4$ tsp
Tomato puree	$^1/_4$ tsp

Garnish

Sweet and sour plum	1 slice

Method
- Soak tomatoes in hot water for 5 minutes then drain. Peel off and discard skin.
- Combine tomatoes and all other ingredients in a blender and puree until fine. Pour into a freezer-proof container and freeze for about 6 hours or until frozen.
- Serve sorbet in a shot glass. Garnish with a slice of sweet and sour plum.

Cabbage
Roll

Ingredients

Chinese cabbage	2 leaves
Ground sesame mustard	1 tsp
Mayonnaise	$^1/_2$ tsp
Pickled snow vegetables	
(*xue cai*)	2 tsp
Ground peanuts	1 tsp
Orange zest	$^1/_2$ tsp
Spring onion (scallion)	2-cm length

Method

- Blanch cabbage then plunge into cold water to stop the cooking process. Drain well.
- Lay cabbage leaves flat and spread with sesame mustard and mayonnaise.
- Spoon snow vegetables over and sprinkle with ground peanuts and orange zest. Place spring onion in the middle and roll up. Slice and serve cold.

Award-Winning
Pork Loin ^{with}
Coffee Sauce

Serves 1

Ingredients

Pork loin	100 g, cut into 2.5-cm pieces
Light soy sauce	$^1/_2$ tsp
Sugar	1 tsp
Sesame oil	a dash
Egg white	1 tsp
Corn flour (cornstarch)	1 tsp
Cooking oil	500 ml

Coffee Sauce

Kahlua	$^1/_2$ tsp
A1 sauce	20 ml
Tomato puree	3 tsp
Plum oil	3 tsp
Apple jam	4 tsp
Salt	$^1/_2$ tsp
Sugar	$^1/_2$ tsp
Instant coffee powder	3 tsp
Water	5 tsp

Garnish

Orange zest
Thyme

Method

- Marinate pork in light soy sauce, sugar, sesame oil, egg white and corn flour and leave overnight. Heat oil and deep-fry marinated pork until cooked.
- Combine coffee sauce ingredients in a pot and cook over low heat until ingredients are well mixed. Remove from heat and leave to cool.
- Reheat coffee sauce just before serving. Spoon over pork. Garnish with orange zest and thyme.

Crispy **Scallops** Wrapped in **White** **Julienned Vegetables** with Sesame Seed Dressing

Serves 1

Ingredients

Scallops	3, medium-size
Carrot	5 g, julienned
Coriander (cilantro)	5 g
Daikon sprouts	5 g
Young green mango	5 g, peeled and julienned

Crispy Scallop Flour (see Chef's Note)

Plain (all-purpose) flour	120 g
Wheat starch flour	30 g
Baking powder	20 g
Custard powder	6 g

Seasoning

Champagne	50 ml
White sesame paste	1 Tbsp
Sesame oil	1/4 tsp
Sugar	1/2 tsp
Mayonnaise	1 tsp
Lemon juice	1 tsp

Method

- Combine crispy scallop flour ingredients and mix well. Take 40 g of it and mix with 40 ml cold water and 1 Tbsp cooking oil into a batter.
- Coat scallops, carrot, coriander, daikon sprouts and green mango in batter and deep-fry until golden brown.
- Combine seasoning ingredients in a wok and heat. Pour over fried scallops and vegetables just before serving.

Chef's Note:

- The crispy scallop flour mixture is good for 10 servings. Store any excess in a clean airtight container for future use.

Crispy Homemade
Black Bean Curd
with Green Mango Salad

Serves 1

Ingredients
Cooking oil for deep-frying

Homemade Black Bean Curd
Sugar-free soy bean milk	1 litre
Salt	1 tsp
Eggs	10
Fermented black bean sauce	150 g, steamed and minced

Green Mango Salad
Brown sugar	50 g
Thai fish sauce	3 Tbsp
Lemon juice	3 Tbsp
Young green mango	20 g, peeled and julienned
Carrot	20 g, julienned
Shallot	20 g, peeled and julienned
Bird's eye chilli	3 g

Method
- Combine soy bean milk, salt and eggs in a mixing bowl and beat well to mix.
- Line a baking tray with plastic wrap. Strain mixture through a sieve onto prepared tray. Top with minced fermented black beans and steam for 20 minutes.
- Leave to cool to room temperature then chill in the refrigerator for 2 hours until firm.
- Cut bean curd into 3 x 3-cm pieces and deep-fry in hot oil until crisp. Drain and arrange on a serving plate.
- Combine brown sugar, fish sauce and lemon juice. Toss with remaining salad ingredients. Arrange salad on top of bean curd to serve.

Chef's Note:
- When steaming the bean curd, do not cover the steamer completely. Leave a small gap to allow some steam to escape. This will ensure that the surface of the bean curd turns out smooth and flat.

Charcoal-grilled
Julienned Beef Salad
with Shredded Cucumber

Serves 1

Ingredients

Sirloin steak	100 g
Shallot	20 g, peeled and minced
Lemon grass	3 g, minced
Torch ginger bud	3 g, minced
Bird's eye chilli	1, minced
Salt	$1/4$ tsp
Cucumber	10 g, julienned
Tomato	3 g, julienned

Seasoning

Thai fish sauce	1 tsp
Honey	2 tsp
Lemon juice	1 tsp
Sesame oil	$1/2$ tsp
Tabasco sauce	$1/4$ tsp
Roasted ground rice*	$1/4$ tsp

Garnish
Roasted white sesame seeds
Chives

Method
- Tenderise steak by roughly chopping with the spine of a cleaver. Marinate with minced shallot, lemon grass, torch ginger bud, bird's eye chilli and salt. Grill over a charcoal fire for 1 minute on each side or to your preferred doneness.
- Julienne steak then marinate with combined seasoning ingredients.
- Arrange cucumber, tomato and beef in a serving container. Sprinkle with sesame seeds and chives.

*Roasted Ground Rice

Ingredients
Raw rice	225 g

Method
- Heat a wok and dry fry rice for 10 minutes until brown and fragrant.
- Grind until fine and leave to cool. Store in an airtight container at room temperature until needed.

Wok-fried
Crab Claw _{with}
Seared Radish Cake
in Black Pepper Sauce

Serves 1

Ingredients

Sri Lankan crab claw	1, soaked in iced water and shelled
Egg	1/4, beaten
Corn flour (cornstarch)	3 g
Cooking oil for deep-frying	

Black Pepper Sauce (see Chef's Note)

Butter	30 g
Garlic	15 g, peeled and minced
Red chillies	15 g, minced
Mint leaves	10 g, minced
Water	200 ml
Ground black pepper	15 g
Maggi seasoning	30 g
Icing (confectioner's) sugar	30 g
Worcestershire sauce	2 tsp
Tomato paste	70 g
Dark soy sauce	150 ml
Plain (all-purpose) flour	10 g

Radish Cake

Water	500 ml
Glutinous rice flour	75 g
Potato flour	20 g
Corn flour (cornstarch)	20 g
Daikon (Japanese radish)	100 g, julienned and stir-fried
Dried prawns (shrimps)	20 g, minced and stir-fried
Fresh shiitake mushrooms	20 g, stir-fried
Chinese sausages	20 g, minced and stir-fried
Sugar	5 g
Salt	5 g
Cooking oil	1 Tbsp

Method

- Prepare black pepper sauce. Heat butter and sauté minced garlic. Add red chillies, mint leaves and water and bring to the boil. Add all remaining ingredients except flour. Mix flour with some water and stir into sauce to thicken. Set aside.
- Prepare radish cake. Mix 250 ml water with glutinous rice flour, potato flour and corn flour. Set aside. Mix remaining water with daikon, dried prawns, mushrooms, Chinese sausages, sugar and salt. Combine both mixtures and pour into a square baking tray. Steam for 35 minutes then leave to cool before cutting into 3 x 3-cm pieces. Heat a pan with a little oil and sear radish cakes until lightly browned. Arrange on a serving plate.
- Coat crab claw with egg and corn flour. Heat oil in a wok and deep-fry claw for about 1 minute until crisp and golden brown.
- Leaving 1 Tbsp oil in wok, heat 3 Tbsp black pepper sauce. Add crab claw and sauté. Arrange on radish cake to serve.

Chef's Note:

- This recipe for black pepper sauce is good for 10 servings. Store any excess in a clean covered container and refrigerate.
- Soaking the crab claw in iced water for 5 minutes will allow the flesh to separate readily from the shell. Simply crack the claw and remove the shell to reveal the flesh.

Crispy Lychee Stuffed with
Crab Meat in Mint Curry Sauce

Serves 1

Ingredients

Cooking oil	1 Tbsp
Onion	20 g, peeled and shredded
Chicken consommé	40 ml (page 24)
Crab meat	40 g
Salt	1/3 tsp
Sugar	1/3 tsp
Curry powder	1/4 tsp
Chinese cooking wine (*hua tiao*)	1 tsp
Fresh or canned lychees	6, pitted
Cooking oil for deep-frying	

Crispy Lychee Flour (see Chef's Note)

Plain (all-purpose) flour	120 g
Wheat starch flour	30 g
Baking powder	20 g
Custard powder	6 g

Mint Curry Sauce

Mint leaves	20 g, minced
Curry powder	1/2 tsp, mixed with 1 Tbsp hot water
Lemon juice	2 tsp
Honey	2 tsp
Salt	1/2 tsp

Method

- Heat oil in a wok and sauté onion until fragrant. Add chicken consommé, crab meat, salt, sugar, curry powder and Chinese cooking wine. Simmer for 5 minutes until mixture is dry. Leave to cool then stuff cooled mixture into lychees.
- Combine crispy lychee flour ingredients and mix well. Take 40 g of it and mix with 40 ml cold water and 1 Tbsp corn oil into a batter.
- Coat stuffed lychee with batter and deep-fry until golden brown.
- Combine mint curry sauce ingredients and drizzle over fried lychees. Serve.

Chef's Note:

- The crispy lychee flour mixture is good for 10 servings. Store any excess in a clean airtight container for future use.

Sesame-coated
Green Asparagus
Wrapped with
Pork Loin

Serves 1

Ingredients

Pork loin	80 g
Shallot	3 g, peeled and minced
Daikon (Japanese radish)	3 g, minced
Torch ginger bud	3 g, minced
Lemon rind	2 g, minced
Asparagus	6 spears
White sesame seeds	5 g
Cooking oil for deep-frying	

Sauce

Teppanyaki sauce	1 tsp
Light soy sauce	1 tsp
Sesame oil	$^1/_4$ tsp
Sugar	2 tsp
Sage	$^1/_4$ tsp
Mirin	$^1/_4$ tsp
Egg white	$^1/_2$

Method

- Simmer pork loin in water for 25 minutes until soft and tender. Leave to cool then slice into 6 thin slices. Marinate with minced shallot, daikon, torch ginger bud and lemon rind. Set aside.
- Blanch asparagus in hot water then plunge into cold water to stop the cooking process.
- Place an asparagus spear on a slice of marinated pork and roll up tightly. Coat with sesame seeds. Continue to make 6 rolls. Heat oil and deep-fry until crisp and golden brown.
- Combine all sauce ingredients except egg white in a wok. Bring to the boil then reduce heat and stir in egg white. Mix well. Serve with asparagus rolls.

Rock and Roll Salad

Ingredients

Mixed salad (rocket, lettuce, daikon sprouts, enoki mushrooms, red cabbage, strawberries, Japanese cucumber and/or tomatoes)	150 g, sliced

Dressing

Lemon juice	20 ml
Mayonnaise	30 g
Salt	1 tsp
Sugar	1 tsp
Tabasco sauce	1 tsp
Olive oil	160 ml

Garnish

Roasted almonds
Roasted cashew nuts
Pine nuts

Method

- Prepare dressing. Mix lemon juice together with mayonnaise, salt, sugar and Tabasco sauce in a blender then pour in olive oil slowly to mix.
- Combine mixed salad with dressing in a jar. Shake well to mix. Arrange salad greens on a plate and garnish with almonds, cashew nuts and pine nuts.

Chef's Note:

- This recipe was named after the way in which the salad is rocked in the jar.

Olive Fried Rice with
Assorted Seafood Sashimi

Serves 1

Ingredients

Salmon	20 g, diced
Tuna	20 g, diced
Prawns (shrimps)	20 g, poached and shelled
Salt	$1/2$ tsp
Sugar	$1/2$ tsp
Sesame oil	$1/4$ tsp
Ground white pepper	a dash
Wasabi	$1/4$ tsp
Light soy sauce	1 tsp
Honey	$1/4$ tsp
Mirin	$1/4$ tsp

Olive Fried Rice

Cooking oil	1 Tbsp
Black olives	10 g, minced
Egg	1
Steamed rice	100 g
Salt	$1/4$ tsp
Sugar	$1/2$ tsp
Ground white pepper	a dash

Garnish

Black ebiko (capelin roe)	
Orange ebiko (capelin roe)	
Quail's egg yolk	1

Method

- Prepare olive fried rice. Heat oil in a wok and sauté black olives until fragrant. Add egg and scramble. Add rice, salt, sugar and pepper. Mix well. Press hot fried rice into a ring cutter to form a rice patty. Set aside.
- Marinate salmon, tuna and prawns with salt, sugar, sesame oil, pepper, wasabi, light soy sauce, honey and mirin. Arrange on top of olive fried rice patty and garnish with ebiko and egg yolk.

Pork Belly ^{with}
Green Asparagus ⁱⁿ
Garlic Vinaigrette

Serves 1

Ingredients

Pork belly	120 g
Asparagus	6 spears
Cooking oil	1 Tbsp

Garlic Vinaigrette

Garlic	5 g, peeled and minced
Japanese sweet barbecue sauce	3 Tbsp
Light soy sauce	3 Tbsp
Dark soy sauce	1/2 Tbsp
Chilli oil	1 Tbsp
Sesame oil	1/2 Tbsp
Honey	2 Tbsp
Fermented red bean paste	1 Tbsp
Black vinegar	2 Tbsp

Garnish
Alfalfa sprouts

Method
- Simmer pork belly in water for 25 minutes until soft and tender. Leave to cool then slice thinly.
- Place asparagus on a slice of pork and roll up tightly. Repeat to make more rolls. Sit rolls on the exposed edge of pork so they do not come undone. Set aside.
- Heat oil in a wok and sauté garlic briefly. And remaining garlic vinaigrette ingredients and heat through. Pour over pork rolls before serving. Garnish with alfalfa sprouts.

Baked Cod Marinated with
Superior Light Soy Sauce
and Honey

Ingredients

Cod fish fillet	100 g

Marinade

Light soy sauce	5 tsp
Water	4 tsp
Dark soy sauce	2 tsp
Sugar	1 tsp
Maggi seasoning	1 tsp

Egg White Garnish

Cooking oil	$^1/_2$ tsp
Chicken consommé	40 ml (page 24)
Salt	$^1/_4$ tsp
Ground white pepper	a dash
Corn flour (cornstarch)	$^1/_2$ tsp mixed with 1 tsp water
Egg white	$^1/_2$

Method

- Combine marinate ingredients. Place cod in to marinate for 15 minutes then transfer cod to a baking tray. Bake cod in an oven at 150°C for 10 minutes. Reduce to 100°C then bake for another 10 minutes.
- Prepare egg white garnish. Heat oil in a wok. Add chicken consommé, salt and pepper then thicken with corn flour mixture. Stir in egg white until cooked.
- Serve cod with egg white garnish.

Steamed **Abalone** with
Fermented **Black Bean** and
Pepper Mint Dressing

Serves 1

Ingredients

Abalone brine from can	
Canned whole abalone	1, about 100 g
Chicken feet	50 g
Pork loin	100 g
Chicken	100 g

Sauce

Cooking oil	1/2 tsp
Fermented black bean sauce	1/3 tsp, minced
Sesame oil	1/4 tsp
Olive oil	1 tsp
Mirin	1/4 tsp
Sake	1/4 tsp
Salt	1/4 tsp
White vinegar	1 tsp
Daikon (Japanese radish)	2 g, grated
Mint leaves	2 g, minced

Method

- Pour brine into a slow cooker and add abalone, chicken feet, pork loin and chicken. Cook for 6 hours until meats are soft and tender. Discard meats except abalone. Leave to cool then chill in the refrigerator. Slice abalone thinly.
- Heat wok and add oil. Fry black beans until fragrant. Add all other sauce ingredients and bring to the boil. Leave to cool.
- Pour cooled sauce over abalone slices to serve.

Seared
Stuffed Chicken
in Cream of Mushroom

Serves 1

Ingredients

Boneless chicken drumstick	1
Salt	$1/4$ tsp
Sesame oil	$1/4$ tsp
Spring onion (scallion)	1
Celery	1 stalk
Bacon	5 g

Cream of Mushroom

Fresh shiitake mushrooms	50 g, minced
Rosemary	1 g
Thyme	1 g
Bay leaves	1 g
Garlic	1 g, peeled and minced
Whipping cream	30 ml
Chicken consommé	100 ml (page 24)

Filling

Prawns (shrimps)	160 g, shelled and minced
Pork loin	60 g, minced
Vegetable shortening	20 g, finely chopped
Dried sole	10 g, baked and finely ground
Fresh shiitake mushrooms	20 g, minced

Seasoning

Salt	$1/2$ tsp
Sugar	$1/2$ tsp
Ground white pepper	a dash
Sesame oil	a dash

Method

- Combine cream of mushroom ingredients and simmer until liquid is reduced. Set aside.
- Combine filling ingredients with seasoning and mix well. Set aside.
- Marinate chicken with salt and sesame oil. Lay chicken flat. Arrange spring onion, celery, bacon and filling on chicken and roll up tightly. Sit roll on exposed edge of chicken so it does not come undone. Steam for 15 minutes until cooked.
- Slice chicken roll into rounds and arrange on a plate.
- Reheat cream of mushroom and pour over chicken rolls.

Steamed **Fillet Pomfret** with
Wood Ear Fungus and
Hon Shimeiji Mushrooms
in **Special Soy Sauce**

Serves 1

Ingredients

Pomfret fillet	120 g
Salt	$^1/_4$ tsp
Sesame oil	$^1/_4$ tsp
Wood ear fungus (*hei mu er*)	5 g
Hon shimeiji mushrooms	10 g
Pickled mustard greens	
(*mei cai*)	10 g
Light soy sauce	$^1/_2$ tsp
Sugar	$^1/_2$ tsp

Special Soy Sauce

Cooking oil	2 Tbsp
Ginger	10 g, peeled and sliced
Spring onion (scallion)	10 g
Chicken consommé	250 ml (page 24)
Light soy sauce	30 ml
Rock sugar	10 g
Dark soy sauce	1 tsp
Coriander (cilantro) leaves	10 g

Garnish

Coriander (cilantro)
Spring onion (scallion)
Red chilli

Method

- Prepare special soy sauce. Heat 1 Tbsp oil in a wok and sauté 2 slices ginger and 5 g spring onion. Add remaining sauce ingredients except coriander. Bring to the boil then leave sauce to cool. Add coriander and set aside.
- Marinate pomfret with salt and sesame oil in a heatproof serving plate. Set aside.
- Clean wok and heat remaining 1 Tbsp oil. Sauté wood ear fungus, hon shimeiji mushrooms and pickled mustard greens with light soy sauce and sugar. Pour over marinated fish and steam for 15 minutes.
- Reheat special soy sauce and pour over steamed fish to serve.

Braised La Mian with Lobster

Serves 1

Ingredients

Shanghainese *la mian*	100 g
Cooking oil	1 Tbsp
Lobster pieces	80 g
Whole garlic	5 g, peeled and roasted
Ginger	3 g, peeled and sliced
Spring onion (scallion)	3 g, chopped
Corn flour (cornstarch)	1 tsp, mixed with 2 tsp water

Seasoning

Saffron chicken consommé	160 ml (page 54)
Sugar	1 tsp
Salt	1/2 tsp
Chinese cooking wine (*hua tiao*)	1 tsp
Ground white pepper	a dash

Method

- Poach *la mian* in hot water for 1 minute until soft. Rinse in cold water and drain. Leave to dry.
- Heat oil in a wok and sauté lobster together with roasted garlic, ginger and spring onion. Add seasoning ingredients and bring to the boil. Add *la mian* and simmer for 2 minutes. Thicken gravy with corn flour.

Baked **Aubergine** Stuffed with
Sautéed Minced Chicken
in **Spicy Hot Bean Sauce**

Serves 1

Ingredients

Japanese aubergines (brinjals/eggplants)	120 g
Salt	1 tsp
Cooking oil	$^1/_2$ tsp
Minced chicken	80 g
Chicken consommé	80 ml (page 24)
Corn flour (cornstarch)	1 tsp, mixed with 2 tsp water

Seasoning

Hot bean sauce	$^1/_2$ tsp
Sesame oil	$^1/_4$ tsp
Oyster sauce	$^1/_2$ tsp
Light soy sauce	$^1/_2$ tsp
Chinese cooking wine (*hua tiao*)	$^1/_2$ tsp
Ground white pepper	a dash

Garnish

Ground peanuts
Minced red chilli
Chervil

Method

- Cut aubergines into 5-cm thick rounds. Scoop out flesh from one cut side with a melon baller.
- Arrange cut aubergines on a baking tray and sprinkle with salt. Steam for 3 minutes.
- Heat oil in a wok and sauté minced chicken until fragrant. Add chicken consommé and seasoning ingredients. Bring to the boil and thicken with corn flour mixture.
- Spoon mixture into aubergines and bake in an oven at 120°C for 5 minutes. Garnish with ground peanuts, minced chilli and chervil.

Shark's Fin Melon and
Nameko Mushrooms
Marinated with
Sesame Light Soy Sauce

Serves 1

Ingredients

Shark's fin melon shreds*	120 g
Nameko mushrooms	30 g, poached
Coriander (cilantro) leaves	5 g
Sesame oil	$1/_2$ tsp
Light soy sauce	1 tsp
Salt	$1/_3$ tsp
White vinegar	$1/_2$ tsp
Chinese cooking wine (hua tiao)	$1/_2$ tsp

Method

- Combine all ingredients and mix well. Serve as an appetiser.

*Shark's Fin Melon Shreds

Ingredients

Shark's fin melon	1

Method

- Cut cap off shark's fin melon. Scrape out and discard seeds.
- Fill with lightly salted water and steam for 20 minutes. Discard water and use a fork to scrape out flesh.

Wok-fried and Stewed
Assorted Mushrooms
with Soy Bean Milk

Serves 1

Ingredients

Cooking oil	1 Tbsp
Hon shimeiji mushrooms	30 g
Fresh shiitake mushrooms	30 g, sliced
Enoki mushrooms	20 g
Button mushrooms	20 g, sliced

Seasoning

Soy bean milk	40 ml
Chicken consommé	40 ml (page 24)
Sour cream	2 tsp
Basil	3 g, minced
Garlic	3 g, minced
Rosemary	3 g
Sugar	1 tsp
Salt	$1/2$ tsp
Ground white pepper	a dash

Garnish

Coriander (cilantro) leaves

Method

■ Heat oil in a wok and sauté mushrooms until fragrant. Add seasoning ingredients and simmer for 10 minutes. Garnish with coriander.

Flowering Cabbage
with Dried Scallops
in Superior Chicken Consommé

Serves 1

Ingredients

Cooking oil	1 Tbsp
Flowering cabbage (*cai xin*)	120 g, chopped and poached
Dried scallops	20 g, steamed and shredded (page 26)
Whole garlic	3 g, roasted
Chicken consommé	160 ml (page 24)
Scallop jus	40 ml (from steaming dried scallops above)
Sugar	1 tsp
Salt	1/4 tsp
Chinese cooking wine (*hua tiao*)	1 tsp
Ground white pepper	a dash

Method

- Heat oil in a wok and sauté flowering cabbage, dried scallops and roasted garlic until fragrant.
- Stir in chicken consommé, scallop jus, sugar, salt, Chinese cooking wine and pepper. Dish out and serve.

Wok-fried Long Beans
with Homemade Dry XO Sauce

Serves 1

Ingredients
Cooking oil for deep-frying

Long beans	120 g, cut into 3-cm lengths

Dry XO Sauce (see Chef's Note)

Icing (confectioner's) sugar	1 Tbsp
Chilli powder	1/2 Tbsp
Chicken stock powder	1/2 Tbsp
Dried scallops	75 g, steamed (page 26), drained and deep-fried
Garlic	35 g, roasted, peeled and minced
Shallots	75 g, roasted, peeled and minced
Chicken floss	75 g
Dried prawns (shrimps)	35 g, roasted and minced
Chinese (Yunnan) ham	250 g, roasted and shredded

Method
- Combine XO sauce ingredients and mix well.
- Heat oil in a wok and deep-fry long beans until crisp. Drain and leave for 2 minutes.
- Leave 1 Tbsp oil in wok and sauté long beans with 5 Tbsp dry XO sauce. Dish out and serve. Top with more dry XO sauce as desired.

Chef's Note:
- This recipe for dry XO sauce is good for 10 servings. Store any excess in an airtight container and keep refrigerated.

Spinach, Cauliflower and Tomato Puree with Walnut

Serves 1

Ingredients

Tomato Puree

Cooking oil	$1/4$ Tbsp
Tomatoes	40 g, poached, skinned and pureed
Chicken consommé	4 tsp (page 24)
Tomato paste	2 tsp
Salt	$1/4$ tsp
Sugar	$1/4$ tsp
Ground white pepper	a dash
Corn flour (cornstarch)	$1/4$ tsp, mixed with 2 tsp water

Cauliflower Puree

Cauliflower	40 g, poached and pureed
Chicken consommé	4 tsp (page 24)
Whipping cream	4 tsp
Cooking oil	$1/4$ Tbsp
Salt	$1/4$ tsp
Sugar	$1/4$ tsp
Ground white pepper	a dash
Corn flour (cornstarch)	$1/4$ tsp, mixed with 2 tsp water

Spinach Puree

Spinach leaves	40 g, poached and pureed
Chicken consommé	4 tsp (page 24)
Cooking oil	$1/4$ Tbsp
Salt	$1/4$ tsp
Sugar	$1/4$ tsp
Ground white pepper	a dash
Corn flour (cornstarch)	$1/4$ tsp, mixed with 2 tsp water

Garnish

Walnuts	5 g, minced

Method

- Prepare tomato puree. Heat oil in a wok. Add tomato puree ingredients except corn flour mixture and bring to the boil. Thicken with corn flour mixture. Repeat steps to make cauliflower and spinach puree.
- Fill a shot glass up to one-third full with tomato puree, then cauliflower puree and lastly spinach puree. Garnish with walnuts.

Whole
Bailing Mushroom with
Sautéed Julienned Snow Peas
and Black Truffle

Serves 1

Ingredients

Bailing mushroom	1, about 80 g
Lean pork	200 g
Chicken	200 g
Chicken feet	100 g
Water	500 ml
Rock sugar	30 g
Dark soy sauce	$^1/_4$ tsp
Chinese (Yunnan) ham	100 g
Cooking oil	1 Tbsp
Snow peas	50 g, julienned and poached
Salt	$^1/_2$ tsp
Black truffle shavings	

Method

- Poach mushroom, pork, chicken, chicken feet and ham in boiling water for about 5 minutes. Rinse with cold water and strain. Place into a pot.
- Add water, rock sugar and dark soy sauce and braise over low heat for 1 hour until sauce is thick and reduced. Discard meats. Set aside mushroom and sauce.
- Heat oil in a wok and sauté snow peas. Season with salt. Arrange mushroom on a serving plate and spoon sauce over. Garnish with snow peas and truffle.

Poached Half-boiled Egg
with Caviar and Ginger Dressing

Serves 1

Ingredients

Egg — 1

Ginger Dressing

Ginger	10 g
Spring onion (scallion)	10 g
Salt	1 tsp
Sugar	1 tsp
Sesame oil	1 tsp
Cooking oil	3 tsp
Ground white pepper	a dash

Garnish

Caviar
Ground nori (dried seaweed)
  (page 50)

Method

- Combine ginger dressing ingredients in a blender and puree until fine. Set aside.
- Half-boil egg. Bring a pot of water to the boil and turn off heat. Place egg in and cover. Leave for 7 minutes. Cut egg in half and drizzle with ginger dressing. Garnish with caviar and sprinkle with ground nori.

Wok-fried
Vermicelli with
Crab Meat and Crab Roe

Serves 1

Ingredients

Crab roe	30 g
Cooking oil	1 Tbsp
Transparent vermicelli (*fen si*)	80 g, soaked in cold water and drained
Chicken consommé	80 ml (page 24)
Crab meat	80 g
Bean sprouts	30 g
Chives	30 g, finely chopped
Salt	$1/4$ tsp
Sugar	$1/4$ tsp
Ground white pepper	a dash

Garnish

Salted egg yolk	1, steamed and minced
Black vinegar	1 tsp

Method

- Poach crab roe in warm water until half-cooked. Drain and set aside.
- Heat oil in a wok, add vermicelli and chicken consommé and simmer. Add crab meat, bean sprouts and chives. Season with salt, sugar and pepper. Add in crab roe and sauté briefly.
- Garnish with egg yolk and serve with black vinegar in a separate saucer.

Crispy **Prawn** Coated with
Durian Mayo

Serves 1

Ingredients
Prawns (shrimps)	120 g
Cooking oil for deep-frying	

Flour for Deep-fried Prawns (see Chef's Note)
Plain (all-purpose) flour	120 g
Wheat starch flour	30 g
Baking powder	20 g
Custard powder	6 g

Durian Mayo Stage 1
Plain (all-purpose) flour	80 g
Custard powder	30 g
Corn flour (cornstarch)	30 g
Milk powder	30 g
Sugar	300 g
Evaporated milk	1 can (388 g)
Water	400 ml

Durian Mayo Stage 2
Durian flesh	480 g
Vegetable oil	150 ml
Whipping cream	80 ml

Garnish
Daikon sprouts
Basil seeds, soaked

Method
- Prepare durian mayo. Combine stage 1 ingredients and mix well. Steam for 25 minutes. Beat in stage 2 ingredients while still hot. Set aside to chill in the refrigerator.
- Combine flour for deep-fried prawns. Take 40 g and mix with 40 ml cold water and 1 Tbsp oil. Coat prawns and heat oil for deep-frying. Deep-fry prawns until crisp and golden.
- Toss prawns in chilled durian mayo and garnish with daikon sprouts and basil seeds to serve.

Chef's Note:
- The flour for deep-fried prawns is good for 10 servings. Store excess in a clean, dry airtight container.

Nyonya-style
Toro Steak

Serves 1

Ingredients

Toro, tuna or salmon fillet	80 g

Nyonya Sauce

Cooking oil	5 Tbsp
Bird's eye chillies	50 g, minced
Red chillies	30 g, minced
Garlic	40 g, peeled and minced
Shallots	50 g, peeled and minced
Ginger	40 g, peeled and minced
Lemon grass	30 g, minced
Torch ginger bud	40 g, minced
Galangal	30 g peeled and minced
Tamarind pulp	50 g
Kalamansi lime juice	20 ml
Coriander powder	$1/2$ tsp
Curry powder	1 tsp
Galangal powder	1 tsp
Water	400 ml
Salt	3 Tbsp
Sugar	6 Tbsp

Garnish

Alfalfa sprouts

Method

- Prepare Nyonya sauce. Heat oil in a wok and add chillies, garlic, shallots, ginger, lemon grass and torch ginger bud. Sauté for 20 minutes until fragrant then add remaining ingredients.
- Grill fillet over a charcoal fire until desired doneness. Drizzle sauce on the side. Garnish with alfalfa sprouts.

Yellow Pumpkin Broth
with Crab Meat and Walnuts   *Serves 1*

Ingredients

Yellow pumpkin	1
Chicken consommé	160 ml (page 24)
Cooking oil	1 Tbsp
Salt	$1/3$ tsp
Sugar	$1/3$ tsp
Sour cream	$1/2$ tsp
Rosemary	5 g, minced
Thyme	5 g, minced
Ground white pepper	a dash
Crab meat	30 g, steamed
Corn flour (cornstarch)	1 tsp, mixed with 2 tsp water

Garnish

Walnuts	5 g, minced
Pink peppercorns	5 g, crushed

Method

- Steam whole yellow pumpkin for 15 minutes until soft. Cut in half and scoop out seeds. Reserve one half for serving.
- Scrape out flesh from other half of pumpkin and blend with chicken consommé.
- Heat oil in a wok and add pumpkin puree and chicken consommé mixture. Bring to the boil and stir in salt, sugar sour cream, rosemary, thyme and pepper.
- Add crab meat then thicken with corn flour. Spoon broth into reserved half of pumpkin. Garnish with walnuts and peppercorns.

Bean Curd Topped with
Baby Anchovies and
Spring Onion

Serves 1

Ingredients

White bean curd	80 g, poached in hot water

Spring Onion Sauce

Ginger	30 g, peeled and pureed
Spring onions (scallions)	30 g, pureed
Salt	1 tsp
Sugar	$1/2$ tsp
Chinese cooking wine (*hua tiao*)	$1/2$ tsp
Sesame oil	2 tsp
Warm cooking oil	2 tsp

Garnish

Anchovies	20 g, deep-fried
Spring onion (scallion)	30 g, finely sliced

Method

- Combine ingredients for spring onion sauce and pour over bean curd. Garnish with anchovies and spring onion.

Braised
Lamb Shank
with Sautéed Edamame Beans
in Garlic Foam

Serves 1

Ingredients

Lamb shank, deboned	60 g
Cooking oil	$^1/_2$ tsp
Edamame beans	40 g
Salt	to taste

Sauce

Carrot	50 g, diced
Celery	50 g, diced
Rosemary	3 g
Thyme	3 g
Bay leaf	1
Chicken consommé	160 ml (page 24)
Salt	$^1/_4$ tsp
Tomato paste	$^1/_4$ tsp
Red wine	2 tsp

Garlic Foam

Garlic	20 g, peeled
Chicken consommé	50 ml (page 24)
Whipping cream	30 g
Salt	$^1/_2$ tsp

Garnish
Pink peppercorns
Chives

Method
- Pan-sear lamb shank until brown on all sides. Place in a pot with sauce ingredients and braise for 1 hour. Reserve shanks but discard other ingredients.
- Deep-dry whole garlic until brown. Steam with chicken consommé for 30 minutes until garlic is soft. Add cream and process mixture in a blender until foamy. Season with salt.
- Heat oil and sauté edamame beans. Sprinkle with salt to taste.
- Place edamame beans on a plate, top with lamb shanks and spoon garlic foam over. Sprinkle with pink peppercorns and chives.

Tuna Mousse with
Light Soy Sauce and Caviar

Serves 1

Ingredients

Tuna fillet	40 g
Minced white onion	3 g
Minced shallots	3 g
Minced coriander stems	3 g

Seasoning

Light soy sauce	$^1/_2$ tsp
Chicken consommé	3 tsp (page 24)
Lemon juice	$^1/_2$ tsp
Vodka	$^1/_3$ tsp
Sake	$^1/_2$ tsp
Mirin	$^1/_2$ tsp

Garnish

Caviar
Chives

Method

- Blend tuna into a paste and mix well with minced ingredients. Place a ring cutter onto a plate and press tuna mixture in to form a round patty.
- Mix seasoning ingredients and pour over tuna patty. Garnish with caviar and chives.

"Nowadays, we have so many more sauces and ingredients available to us... we can use them to create new dishes."

Glossary

Chinese (Yunnan) ham
This Chinese ham is one of the most well-known hams from China. It is dry-cured and has a thin skin and strong aroma. Good quality Chinese hams retain their flavour well and can be stored for long periods of time.

Foie gras paste
Foie gras is the general term used in reference to duck liver. Foie gras paste is also known as foie gras puree and it is made from goose liver and other ingredients such as pork liver and truffle.

Dried scallops
Also known as conpoy, these are dried sea scallops. Available in various sizes and varying in quality, dried scallops are usually added to steamed or stewed dishes to enhance flavour. Dried scallops can keep indefinitely if stored in an airtight container in a cool, dry place.

Dried sole
This dried fillet of sole fish has a fragrant aroma and is used for flavouring dishes. Bake then grind or pound to use as a powder.

Dried sea olive
Different from Mediterranean olives, the dried sea olive is commonly used in Chinese desserts. It is soaked in water after which a brown jelly will be produced. Remove and discard the skin, then drain and use the jelly.

Rock sugar
As its name suggests, rock sugar comes in large irregularly shaped crystals. It is not as sweet as granulated sugar and is commonly used to sweeten Chinese desserts and soups.

Sweet and sour plum
Commonly eaten as a snack in Asia, these preserved plums have a pleasant sweet-sour taste and can be added to desserts for a unique flavour.

Basil seeds (*selasih*)
These small black oval-shaped seeds are commonly used in desserts. Soaked in water, a transparent jelly-like film forms around each seed. They are favoured for their crunchy texture.

Chinese wolfberries (*gou qi zi*)

Also known as boxthorne berries, Chinese wolfberries are sold dried. They have a mild, sweet taste and can be eaten raw, although they are usually boiled in soups and tonics.

Lotus leaf

The large rounded leaves of the lotus plant, lotus leaves are commonly used in Asian cooking for their flavour. It also acts an environment-friendly disposable food wrapper.

Fragrant Solomonseal rhizome (*yu zhu*)

This Chinese herb is sold thinly sliced. It is believed to be good for the lungs and stomach.

Spring roll wrappers (*popiah* skin)

These are thin skins made from rice flour dough. They are traditionally handmade and come round, but are today available machine-made and come as square sheets. They can be frozen but should be well-thawed before use. Keep unused wrappers wrapped in plastic or covered with a damp cloth to prevent drying out.

Chinese celery
Although it is similar in appearance to continental parsley, Chinese celery is stronger in flavour. It is commonly used to flavour dishes.

Daikon (Japanese radish)
Larger than the Asian white radish but sweeter, the daikon has crisp, juicy and white flesh. It can be eaten raw or cooked. If unavailable, use Chinese radish.

Daikon cress (*kaiware*)
Sprouts grown from the seeds of daikon, these delicate sprouts are used as garnish and are always eaten raw.

Edamame beans
These green coloured beans come two or three in a pod. The beans are cooked in their pods which are then discarded. Edamame beans are available fresh or frozen. They are usually steamed or boiled in lightly salted water and eaten as a snack.

Lemon grass
A long lemon-scented grass popularly used for flavouring curries and soups in Southeast Asia. Only the pale lower portion of the bulbous stem, with the tough outer layers peeled away, is used for cooking.

Galangal
Also known as greater galangal, this rhizome has a delicate and distinctive flavour and is commonly used in curries. It can be added to dishes sliced or pounded/ground.

Kaffir lime leaves
These glossy dark green leaves are easily recognisable as they look like two leaves joined end to end. They have a fragrant lemon flavour and can be used whole or shredded.

Screwpine (*pandan*) leaf
Also known as pandanus leaf, these long narrow leaves have a pronounced spine running down its middle. They have a delicate flavour and are commonly used to wrap and flavour food in Asia. The leaves can be added whole to dishes then removed and discarded before serving, or pounded to extract its juice and colour.

Shark's fin melon (*yu chi gua*)

When cooked, the flesh of this melon separates into fine transparent strips that look very much like glass noodles or cooked shark's fin, hence its name. It has a mild melon flavour and takes on the flavour of the stock it is placed in readily.

Spring onions (scallions)

With long, green, hollow leaves and a bulbous white base, spring onions have a mild onion flavour that is only more pronounced at the bulbous end. Discard any yellowing leaves and cut off the roots before use. Often used as a garnish.

Taro

This dense root-vegetable is oval-shaped with hairy dark brown skin. Rings encircle its hairy skin. The flesh is greyish purple and starchy like the potato.

Torch ginger bud

The bud of this wild ginger has a delicate and refreshing aroma. For cooking purposes, the bud is picked while still tightly folded. Slice finely and add raw to salads for a lovely pink colour and intriguing aroma.

Yellow pumpkin

Also known as Oriental squash, this variety of pumpkin is much smaller than its Western counterpart. It has green skin and sweet yellowish-orange flesh.

Fermented black bean sauce (above left)

This dark coloured sauce with fermented soy beans adds a distinctive earthy flavour to stir-fries or steamed dishes. It is sold in bottles with the beans whole or minced. The whole beans may also be minced before use for greater flavour.

Yellow bean sauce (above right)

This brown coloured sauce with preserved soy beans has a salty flavour and is very popular in Southeast Asian cooking. It is sold in bottles with the beans whole or mashed. The whole beans may also be mashed before use for greater flavour.

Yellow chives

Also known as garlic chives, this variety is cultivated in the dark and so are pale yellow in colour. The leaves are long, limp and flat. Cut off the bottom stems and discard before use. Rinse well and shake dry. Use soon after purchase, as yellow chives do not keep well.

Bailing mushroom
This large mushroom originates from the deserts of northwest China but is now cultivated under controlled conditions. It has an average weight of 100 g and an average diameter of 8–10 cm.

Enokitake mushrooms
Also known by its shortened form, enoki. These thin stemmed mushrooms with small caps grow wild but are today cultivated. Cut off the spongy root then wash thoroughly. Enokitake mushrooms can be eaten cooked or raw. It is enjoyed for its delightful crisp texture.

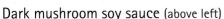

Dark mushroom soy sauce (above left)
Originating from China, this dark soy sauce is flavoured with straw mushrooms. Use as you would other types of soy sauce, as a seasoning or table condiment. It can also be used in place of other soy sauces for a deeper, richer flavour.

Plum oil (above right)
This oil is derived from the kernel of plums. It has a mild plum flavour and a clear golden brown colour.

Nameko mushrooms

Enjoyed for its fungus flavour and sweet taste, nameko mushrooms are only available preserved in brine because of its short shelf life. They have small caps that average 1–2 cm in diameter and are recognisable from the gelatinous substance in which they are coated.

Hon shimeiji mushrooms (white and brown)

This mushroom is mild in flavour but has a meaty texture similar to the oyster mushroom. It is commonly used in soups, or grilled or fried. To use, cut off the hard base then wash briskly.

Wood ear fungus (*hei mu er*)

This dried black fungus should be soaked in water to soften before use. It is prized for its crunchy texture, but is bland with no taste of its own.

Weights & Measures

Quantities for this book are given in Metric and American (spoon) measures. Standard spoon measurements used are: 1 tsp = 5 ml and 1 Tbsp = 15 ml. All measures are level unless otherwise stated.

LIQUID AND VOLUME MEASURES

Metric	Imperial	American
5 ml	$1/6$ fl oz	1 teaspoon
10 ml	$1/3$ fl oz	1 dessertspoon
15 ml	$1/2$ fl oz	1 tablespoon
60 ml	2 fl oz	$1/4$ cup (4 tablespoons)
85 ml	$2^1/2$ fl oz	$1/3$ cup
90 ml	3 fl oz	$3/8$ cup (6 tablespoons)
125 ml	4 fl oz	$1/2$ cup
180 ml	6 fl oz	$3/4$ cup
250 ml	8 fl oz	1 cup
300 ml	10 fl oz ($1/2$ pint)	$1^1/4$ cups
375 ml	12 fl oz	$1^1/2$ cups
435 ml	14 fl oz	$1^3/4$ cups
500 ml	16 fl oz	2 cups
625 ml	20 fl oz (1 pint)	$2^1/2$ cups
750 ml	24 fl oz ($1^1/5$ pints)	3 cups
1 litre	32 fl oz ($1^3/5$ pints)	4 cups
1.25 litres	40 fl oz (2 pints)	5 cups
1.5 litres	48 fl oz ($2^2/5$ pints)	6 cups
2.5 litres	80 fl oz (4 pints)	10 cups

OVEN TEMPERATURE

	°C	°F	Gas Regulo
Very slow	120	250	1
Slow	150	300	2
Moderately slow	160	325	3
Moderate	180	350	4
Moderately hot	190/200	370/400	5/6
Hot	210/220	410/440	6/7
Very hot	230	450	8
Super hot	250/290	475/550	9/10

LENGTH

Metric	Imperial
0.5 cm	$1/4$ inch
1 cm	$1/2$ inch
1.5 cm	$3/4$ inch
2.5 cm	1 inch

DRY MEASURES

Metric	Imperial
30 grams	1 ounce
45 grams	$1^1/2$ ounces
55 grams	2 ounces
70 grams	$2^1/2$ ounces
85 grams	3 ounces
100 grams	$3^1/2$ ounces
110 grams	4 ounces
125 grams	$4^1/2$ ounces
140 grams	5 ounces
280 grams	10 ounces
450 grams	16 ounces (1 pound)
500 grams	1 pound, $1^1/2$ ounces
700 grams	$1^1/2$ pounds
800 grams	$1^3/4$ pounds
1 kilogram	2 pounds, 3 ounces
1.5 kilograms	3 pounds, $4^1/2$ ounces
2 kilograms	4 pounds, 6 ounces

ABBREVIATION

tsp	teaspoon
Tbsp	tablespoon
g	gram
kg	kilogram
ml	millilitre

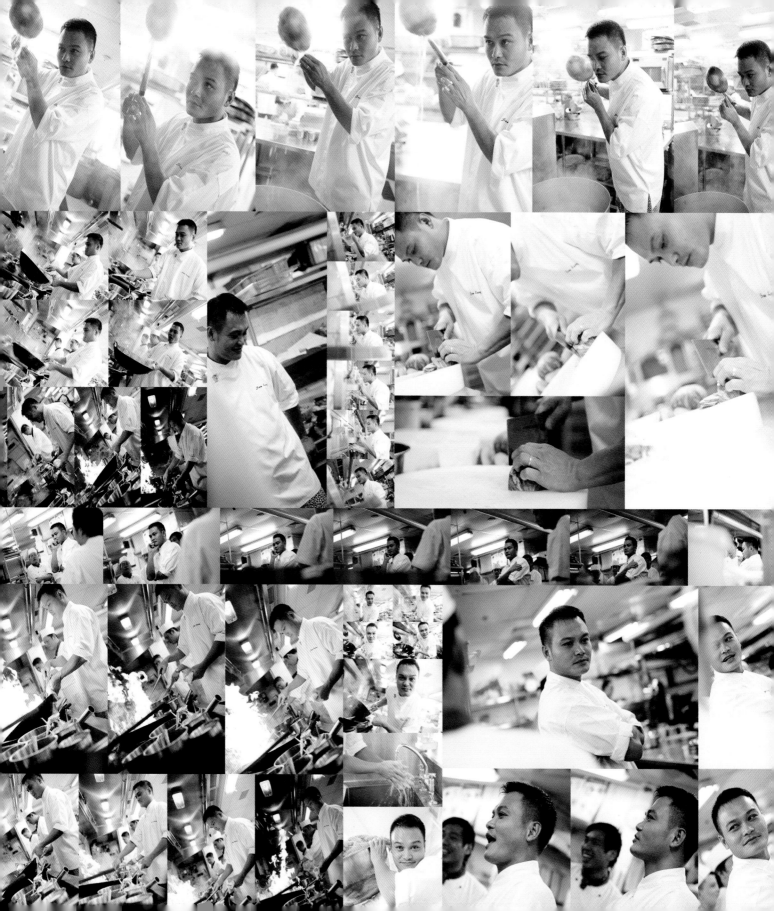

Special thanks to:

Chef Krisna B.
Chef Thomas Chai
David Yip
Lydia Leong
Ang Lee Ming
Peter Knipp
Joyce Choo
Tung Lok Group of Restaurants